The
Garden

The
Garden

A SPIRITUAL FABLE ABOUT
WAYS TO **OVERCOME FEAR,**
ANXIETY, AND **STRESS**

JON GORDON

WILEY

To Erwin McManus. I am eternally grateful to you.

Contents

Contents

Introduction

Warning!

I felt I should put a warning label on this book because I'm known as a writer of business fables, and this is not a business fable. This is very different than my other books. This is a spiritual fable rooted in my faith and it addresses the growing epidemic of fear, anxiety, and stress that are affecting millions of people around the world. Having worked with countless leaders, companies, sports teams, and professional athletes I've had intimate conversations and advised many who struggle with fear, stress, and anxiety. I've also spoken at numerous events for college and high school students and have talked with and encouraged many who have reached out the last few years. I've shared the principles and concepts in this book with them and have seen how it has helped them understand and win the battle of their mind.

With that said, even though a lot of mental health experts, counselors, and sports psychologists read and share my books I want you to know that I don't consider myself a mental health expert. And even though people who read my books say it helps their mental health I want to make it clear that this book should not be a substitute for seeing a counselor or getting professional help in dealing with fear, stress, and anxiety. I appreciate the role that mental health experts and counselors play in working with their clients to overcome their mental health challenges.

My goal in writing this is to help people understand the mental battle they are facing from a spiritual perspective. "Psyche" means soul and in many cases, our minds don't need fixing. Rather our soul needs healing. I personally struggled with depression and anxiety in my life and as I nourished my soul and fed my mind with meditation, prayer, and spiritual truths I found more peace, joy, and healing. A big part of this healing was sermons from Erwin McManus who brought Jesus to life for me when I was 35 years old. Erwin helped me realize that you can't win a spiritual battle with man-made strategies. You win it with a greater source of power, truth, and strength. It's the same with 12 step programs and why they all include a higher power.

A few years ago, while walking the streets of downtown Chicago before a talk to a group of business leaders, the 5 D's that I share in this book came to me, like a software download, and I began typing them into my phone. I clearly saw the battle we face and the plan to win the battle and knew I had to write and share this book to help more people overcome their fear, stress, and anxiety.

Is this book the only answer to solve the mental health epidemic? Of course not. The more we learn about the microbiome, (bacteria in our intestines) the more we learn how nutrition and gut health influence mental health. For years studies have shown that exercise and sleep are big factors in one's mood and mindset and new research is helping us understand how loneliness, isolation, and technology all play a role in our mental health. There are many contributing factors that influence how we think and feel on a daily basis and we need a holistic comprehensive approach that involves the mind, body, and spirit to help those who are struggling.

My hope with this book is to share a powerful perspective and paradigm that can be a part of the solution. You may not agree with the faith tradition from which these ideas originate but I believe you will find the 5 D's and practical strategies I share helpful. Whether you are dealing with fear, stress, and anxiety yourself; have a family member that struggles; or are a mental health expert that works with clients, if any of the ideas in this book can be useful to you or the people you love and care about, then I believe it's worthwhile to take a look.

In this spirit let's take a walk through *The Garden* and learn a spiritual paradigm combined with practical strategies to overcome fear, stress, and anxiety. I hope this story fills you with more faith, love, and hope so you can live with more peace and joy.

God bless you,

Jon

The
Garden

Chapter 1

Fears and Secrets

Jay and Kay walked past Mr. Erwin's house on their way to school each day. He had known them since they were babies, coached their youth soccer team, and watched them grow up as a neighbor and family friend.

There was a streetlight in front of his house and as Jay and Kay waited for the signal to cross the street, Mr. Erwin often greeted them while sitting on the front porch drinking his coffee. With his own children grown and on their own, he missed those days when they were in school and enjoyed seeing the twins and their brief conversations where he received updates of how they were doing. Kay had made the cheering team, was nominated for homecoming queen, and was obsessed about her grades and getting an academic scholarship to college. Jay loved being in the school's marching band, making short films with his friends, and was happy with his straight Bs in school. Mr. Erwin was thrilled to hear that everything was going so well. They had always been good kids and it was gratifying to see them thrive as young adults.

Everything was great, or so he thought . . . until that time he badly sprained his ankle and had to sit on the couch by the front window for a week icing it. He wasn't able to greet the twins, but he heard them talk as they waited to cross the street. It was then he found out how much they were struggling.

Twins are known to be connected and share things with each other they wouldn't normally share with others. Jay and Kay were no exception. They talked about everything, and on their walk to school they talked about their innermost fears and darkest secrets; Mr. Erwin overheard snippets that made his heart ache as much as his ankle.

Underneath Kay's excitement about making the cheer team was a fear the size of Texas that she would mess up in front of thousands of people in the audience. And while she was nominated for homecoming queen, she didn't think she was pretty or popular enough to be considered. Jay encouraged her, as he always did, but she didn't see what he or others saw in her. And she was terrified of not getting into her dream school. What would happen if she worked as hard as she possibly could and it still wasn't good enough? She had trouble sleeping because of all the anxiety and started drinking a lot of coffee to get through the day.

Jay, on the other hand, didn't care much about school. He did care about his future but often felt hopeless about it. He was tired of being bullied by classmates who called him band geek and film boy and made it a point to knock into him while walking in the hallways between classes. With each passing day the stories Mr. Erwin heard got worse. One day, they punched Jay. The next day they hid his instrument when he went to the bathroom during class. The day after that they made fun of him in front of a girl he liked.

Fears and Secrets

It was getting to the point Jay didn't want to go to school and revealed to Kay that he didn't want to live anymore. No one cared about his love of music or appreciated his ability to make movies. What was the point, he wondered. Kay made him promise he wouldn't do something they would regret.

"I couldn't live without you," she said as she lifted her long-sleeved shirt to reveal the cut marks she had given herself. "See these cuts," she said. "This is how stressed I am. But I would never end it all. I wouldn't do that to you, so don't do that to me."

Mr. Erwin heard the worst of it on a Friday and knew that Monday he would be back on the front porch to greet them whether his ankle was healed or not.

The Garden

Chapter 2

The Garden

Mr. Erwin sat on his front porch with his crutches by his side. His ankle was feeling better, but he still couldn't walk on it. His wife used to tell him all the time to watch his step. His weak ankles always seemed to find the one hole, uneven road, or short step that would cause his ankle to turn. He sure did miss her. Cancer might have taken her life, but her love still lived deeply in his heart and he thought about her every day. She loved to garden in the backyard and after she passed, he decided to make it his passion. It became a labor of love and an expression of his love for her.

When the twins arrived in front of his house, he greeted them.

"Hey Mr. Erwin," said Kay. "Where have you been? We missed seeing you last week."

"Oh, I've been icing and trying to heal my ankle," he said as he got up from his chair, grabbed his crutches, and hopped down the stairs on one leg towards them. "Sprained it the other day walking out of the store. Haven't been able to work in my garden either and I was wondering if you two could help me real quick. I know you have to get to school but it will only take a few minutes."

Jay and Kay looked at each other. "Sure, we can help," Jay said. "What do you want us to do?"

"Follow me," said Mr. Erwin as he used both crutches to propel himself towards the backyard. "I just need you to unwind the watering hose and move it to the center of the backyard so I can water my trees."

As they approached the backyard, Jay and Kay stopped for a moment and looked at each other. They didn't say it but they were both thinking the same thing. *Are you seeing what I'm seeing?*

The backyard was much larger than expected and it was filled with the most beautiful fruit trees they had ever seen. The trees formed a circle surrounding the perimeter of the property with only a small gap for the entrance to the yard. The early sunlight was glistening off the leaves as ripe, plump fruit dangled from the branches. In the center of the circle was an open space with finely manicured short green grass, a bench, and two trees that stood side by side.

They walked to the center and stood in front of the two trees.

"This is beautiful," said Kay as she nervously tapped her right foot.

"Thank you," Mr. Erwin answered. "It's a special place. I put a lot of work into it."

"Why are these two trees by themselves," asked Jay, who stood with his shoulders slumped.

"I'm glad you asked that," Mr. Erwin said as he sat down on the bench. "I want to tell you an ancient story about a garden that I imagine looked much like this. It was the Garden where God placed a young man and woman named Adam and Eve. In the middle of the Garden He planted two trees: the Tree of Knowledge

11

The Garden

of Good and Evil and the Tree of Life. Do you remember the story?"

"Sort of," said Jay. "It's been a while since I learned about it in Sunday school."

"They ate the fruit of the tree when they weren't supposed to, right?" asked Kay as she continued tapping her foot.

"Yes, but before that part, God showed them all the trees in the Garden," Mr. Erwin said as he pointed to the trees surrounding them, "And God told them that they were free to eat from all these trees, except they were not to eat from one tree, the Tree of Knowledge of Good and Evil that stood next to the Tree of Life. He told them that to eat from this one tree meant that they will die. Then one day a serpent appeared and convinced Eve and Adam to eat from the forbidden tree. As a result of their disobedience, they were banished from the Garden."

Mr. Erwin continued, "I tried to re-create the beauty of the Garden of Eden, including the two trees right here in front of you. When I sit out here and look at these two trees and all the trees in my garden, I am reminded of so many important life lessons." He looked at his watch. "Oh, but you must get to school, so we'll save those lessons for another day. I don't want you to be late, so for now I have just one question to ask you. Why did they eat the fruit? If God told Adam and Eve not to eat from the one tree, why did they do so? I'll share the answer with you tomorrow if you want to know. The answer is not what most people think."

Chapter 3

Identity

The next day Kay and Jay walked and talked as they made their way towards school and Mr. Erwin's house. They thought it was a little strange that he had created a garden like that in his backyard and yet they were compelled to see it again. It was beautiful and mysterious, and they wanted to know why Eve and Adam ate the fruit. They googled it and found most people believed that they ate the fruit because of pride, because they wanted to be like God. When they approached Mr. Erwin's house, they saw him standing by the streetlight with his crutches.

"So, do you want to know why they ate the fruit?" Mr. Erwin asked as they walked towards the backyard.

"They ate it because of pride," said Jay.

"Because they wanted to be like God," said Kay as she and Jay followed Mr. Erwin to the two trees in the center of the Garden.

When they were in front of the two trees, Mr. Erwin put down his crutches and pulled a piece of fruit from the forbidden tree. He told them, "That's what most people think. They think they ate the fruit because they wanted to be like God. But the truth is, earlier in the story we learn that God made human beings in his own likeness and image. This means they didn't eat the fruit because they wanted to be like God because **they already were like God.** They ate the fruit because the serpent convinced them that they weren't like God and they believed this lie.

Mr. Erwin paused and looked at their faces to make sure they understood the magnitude of what he was saying.

He continued, "The serpent caused them to question and forget their identity of who they truly were. Here, they were children of God made in his image and were already like God, and the serpent attacked them at the heart and core of this truth. They were attacked in the place of their identity. As a result of believing the lie and choosing to eat the fruit instead of trusting and following God and remembering who they were, they were then separated from God."

"How come they forgot who they were?" Jay asked with his shoulders still slumped. He couldn't take his eyes off the fruit in Mr. Erwin's hand.

"That's a great question," said Mr. Erwin. "I think we can ask the same question about ourselves too. You see the story of Adam and Eve in the Garden is not just a story about them. It's a story about us. God made us in His image and yet we often believe the lie that we are less than and not enough. We believe that we aren't worthy. We forget that we are children of God.

"Let me ask you both a question. Do you want to be great?"

"Yes, I do," Kay shouted. Her legs stood firm as she said it.

"I want to be a great musician and filmmaker," yelled Jay. "But I don't want to be great at school."

Mr. Erwin chuckled. "That's fine," he said. "We don't always want to be great at everything, but the big question is why do you and everyone else have a desire to be great? Why do we as a species always strive to do more and create more? We go to the moon and then we want to go to Mars. We design and build a car and we want to make an even better car. A musician has a hit song and they want to create another hit. An athlete achieves a remarkable feat and wants to improve upon it the next season. We get a good grade on a test and we want to do even better the next time. We make a great movie and we want to make an even better movie. Where does this desire come from?"

Jay and Kay shrugged.

Mr. Erwin threw the fruit in his hand towards the back of the yard and continued, "I'm convinced you want to be great because God put this desire in your soul. If you are made in His likeness and image then this means there is greatness within you.

God is great and so he planted seeds of greatness in you. God is good so there is goodness in you. God is love so there is love within you.

"Deep down you know this to be true and yet too often you believe the lies that you aren't great. You believe you aren't loved and you are less than. To answer why Adam and Eve forgot who they were we have to ask ourselves, why do we forget who we are? Why do we have a desire for greatness and a knowing at times that we are here to do great things and then at other times we have such feelings of insecurity and unworthiness?"

"Because we aren't perfect," said Kay. "Because we are like God but not God. We make mistakes."

"That's a big part of it," answered Mr. Erwin. "We aren't God. We do fall short of perfection. But why do we make mistakes and bad choices? I believe a big clue can be found in our thoughts.

"Since you have to get to school, let's continue the conversation tomorrow. But before you go, I have a question for you both to ponder and it is this: Do your negative thoughts come from you?"

Chapter 4

Good versus Evil

The next day Mr. Erwin sat on the bench in the garden waiting for Jay and Kay. He knew all those who want to know the truth must seek the truth, and when they came back to the garden by themselves, he knew they were ready to hear it. He was going to ask them about their day at school yesterday but decided that it didn't matter what challenges and situations they were facing. Whatever the challenge was it was just a symptom, a symptom of a deeper cause. Humans experience many different symptoms, such as addictions, fears, stress, anxiety, insecurity, and destructive behavior that are all tied to one root cause. The key was to help people understand and heal the cause of the symptom and the symptom would disappear.

Jay and Kay stood in front of Mr. Erwin, who stayed sitting on the bench with his crutches by his side.

"We think our negative thoughts come from ourselves and other people," said Kay. She was still wearing a long-sleeved shirt to hide the cuts on her arm and tapped her foot on the ground as she talked. "People say negative things to us throughout our lives and then those thoughts become something we think on our own."

"But if negative thoughts come from others, then where did the first negative thought come from?" asked Mr. Erwin. "How did the first person have a negative thought in the first place if it came from someone else? Also, why do people who grow up in 100% positive and supportive households and communities still have negative thoughts? And how come some people listen to the negative thoughts of others and some don't?"

Jay was a little confused. "So it starts with us then," he said. "That's what I think. I can hear the negative thoughts in my head and I know they are from me."

Mr. Erwin shook his head and responded, "If you believe that your negative thoughts come from you, ask yourself this question. Who would ever choose to have a negative thought? I wouldn't choose one. Would you?"

"No," Jay said.

"I wouldn't choose one," Kay responded.

"No one would choose a negative thought, so where do they come from?" asked Mr. Erwin.

"I have no idea," said Jay, shaking his head with his shoulders slumped as usual. "I'm lost."

"Thoughts are spiritual, not physical," said Mr. Erwin. "No one has ever found a thought in their brain. It's not a physical thing. Your brain is the hardware. Thoughts exist like software in the internet cloud and are always being downloaded. Thoughts are always coming in just like dreams and nightmares do when we are sleeping. You don't choose your dreams and nightmares do you," he asked?

Jay and Kay said "no" in unison while shaking their heads side to side.

"Thoughts are spiritual," Mr. Erwin reiterated. "There's a spiritual battle going on between good and evil. We see this taking place in the world with killings and shootings, kidnappings, bombings, and other evil acts and we need to know that the battleground between good and evil begins in our heart, mind, and soul."

"It's like the movies," said Jay as he arched his back and stood up straight. "*Star Wars, Black Panther, Superman, Wonder Woman, Harry Potter,* are all stories of good versus evil."

"You nailed it, Jay," said Mr. Erwin. "Every epic story is a story of good versus evil. These movies resonate so much with us because the same battle we see on the movie screen is what we are experiencing in our soul and in the world. It's the major narrative in the universe and in our existence. Most believe in evil because they see it but they can't explain where it comes from. They tend to focus on the person committing an evil act. Many think evil comes from our human nature, but it is actually spiritual in nature. What people need to realize is there is an evil force that exists and is part of the fabric of our existence."

"But why?" Jay blurted out as he looked at the forbidden tree. "Why does evil exist at all? I mean why did God even allow Adam and Eve to have a choice? Why couldn't it all just be good?"

"You just asked the question that the greatest thinkers, scholars, and theologians have asked since the beginning of time. I'm no scholar but I think God is the ultimate storyteller, and in every story, you must have conflict and struggle. You must have duality. Love and hate. Light and dark. Good and evil. Defeat and victory. You wouldn't know good without bad. You wouldn't know it was light unless you have experienced the dark.

"You're a moviemaker, Jay. Tell me what kind of movie would it be if the characters didn't make bad and good choices? Would there be any victory or triumph without struggle, conflict, and defeat along the way?"

"No," said Jay emphatically. "There are key elements to every great story and the main character must make choices and evolve and we must see their transformation as they go through their struggle and face their conflict."

"It's all about choices and transformation," said Mr. Erwin. "At God's level there is no duality. It's all oneness. It's all love. It's all good. When he created our world, he created a world of duality in order to tell a story where we can make choices and have us experience and live out this story.

"To answer your question of why Adam and Eve were given a choice in the first place, they had to be given a choice. God had to create space for them to choose Him."

Mr Erwin stopped for a moment then took a deep breath. He wanted the twins to truly grasp what he was about to say. He spoke a little slower, yet with more passion.

"Evil is the absence of God. This means that in the space between Man and God, evil exists. And this space is necessary because God had to give us a choice. He had to give us space to choose to love and obey Him. True love doesn't demand to be loved back. True love is freely given and the recipient is given a choice to love in return. If there was no choice and it was all good all the time, there would be no world, no story, and no us."

It finally made sense to Jay. He said, "So there's a major narrative and story playing out on the movie screen of the universe and it is both the ultimate love story and epic battle between good and evil."

"Yes," responded Mr. Erwin. "Before there was *Star Wars* and *Harry Potter* there was God, Adam and Eve, and a serpent. And the story continues with us. God has a plan for our lives. He created us to be in partnership with Him. He made us in his likeness and image. He created us to live a life of goodness, love, and abundance. But then there is evil that exists in the space between us and God and it seeks to mislead us, to separate us from God, to destroy us, and to keep us from living the life God has created us to live.

"We have a choice," said Kay. "I love that we have a choice. Life would be meaningless without it."

"It is the ultimate choice, responded Mr. Erwin. You can choose to love and obey God and overcome evil with good or you can believe the lie and let evil win. It's a battle between good and evil and you are in the middle of it."

"It's scary to know this," said Kay.

"I agree," said Mr. Erwin. "That's why it's not popular to talk about it. It's easier to ignore it, to pretend this isn't happening or be unmindful that it is happening. But when so many people, especially young people like you, are stressed, fearful, anxious, and even committing suicide, it's scarier not to talk about it. Look around and you'll see so many losing the battle. It's scarier to see all these people suffer, and they have no clue what's really going on and why they are really suffering. It's scarier to see so many clutter the problem with complexity by focusing on all the symptoms instead of understanding and focusing on the root cause. **It's scarier to see so many losing a battle they have no idea they are in. If you don't know**

you are in a battle but your enemy does, you will surely lose.

"That's what's happening more frequently today. The battle has become more intense and is including more people, and they have no idea they are in a battle. So they are getting beat down on a daily basis. They think life is a playground but need to approach it like it's a battleground. When you know you are in a battle then you can win it. That's why I'm being so blunt about this."

"How do you win the battle?" asked Jay. He felt like he was battling for his life every day at school and wanted to win for once.

"You have to know how the battle is being waged," said Mr. Erwin. "That's why tomorrow I want to share with you the Five D's that evil uses to defeat you. Yesterday you asked how come Adam and Eve forgot who they were. I believe it's because evil used these Five D's to cause them to forget who they were and disobey God. These are the same Five D's evil continues to use to cause us to forget our identity so that evil can defeat us.

"In the story of Adam and Eve, evil uses a Serpent to be our enemy. In our story we face an enemy as well. Many call him the devil, but whatever you want to call him, he is crafty like the serpent and he has a plan to defeat you. I'm sharing these Five D's with you because they represent evil's only game plan to attack you. Once you know evil's game plan, you can counter it and win the battle.

"I am here to help you win the battle and once you do you will live the amazing life that God has for you."

Chapter 5

Doubt

The next day Mr. Erwin was watering the trees in his garden with his crutches by his side when Kay and Jay arrived. It was extra hot for a fall morning but that didn't stop Kay from wearing a long-sleeved shirt. Jay's left eye was black and blue and he had a cut on his left knuckle. Mr. Erwin knew all too well that spiritual battles turn into physical battles. He wished he could go to school and deal with the boys messing with Jay, but just like with his own son, he knew Jay would have to fight his own battle and learn how to win in order to grow.

"What's the first D?" asked Kay. "Jay and I have been trying to figure it out all morning."

Mr. Erwin smiled. He loved that they weren't scared but rather eager to learn the enemy's game plan. Because once they learned the Five D's, he would be able to teach them how to overcome them and win.

He said, "The first D is Doubt. The enemy begins his quest to defeat you by creating doubt that God can't be trusted. If you read the story of Adam and Eve, you'll see that when the serpent first started talking to Eve he asked, 'Did God really say that you couldn't eat from all the trees in the Garden?' The truth was that God said they couldn't eat from just that one tree. But by asking this question, the enemy was creating doubt in the mind of Eve that God can't be trusted, that He was withholding the best from them.

"Today the enemy plants seeds of doubt in our mind all the time. You see others doing well and thriving and you wonder why they are doing so well but you aren't. You see others achieve their dream while yours seems more like a fantasy than a reality. You see others having success and you feel like a failure. You wonder if God likes them more than you, and you begin to resent God and lose trust in Him. God gave Adam and Eve a choice and

His central question of them and us is this: will you trust me? The enemy's main goal is to break this trust by creating doubt."

Mr. Erwin placed the watering hose on the ground. "Is this making sense?" he asked as he wiped his hands on his pants to get the water and dirt off.

"I doubt myself all the time," said Jay. "I don't think I'll ever make it as a musician or filmmaker. And I guess I doubt God for making me the way He did." He looked at the cut on his hand, "Why do I have to be the one who is bullied?"

"Self-doubt ironically doesn't come from self. Remember that," said Mr. Erwin. "God made you perfectly and you are the way you are for a reason and a purpose. The fact that you doubt who you are and your future means the enemy is filling your mind with doubt. You would never do that to yourself. Your identity is being attacked and the bullying is a painful experience that is reinforcing this doubt and causing you to forget you are a child of God."

"I have all these doubts about my ability to do well in cheering, said Kay. "I worry I'm going to make a mistake. I worry people will find out I'm not really that good. I worry I'm going to let my coaches and team down."

"That's because the enemy is filling your mind with these doubts and fears, said Mr. Erwin. You would never choose doubt so remember these doubts aren't coming from you. These doubts appear and then you feel like you must be perfect to compensate. You don't trust God so you try to be perfect like God. But you aren't perfect and you know this and it causes a lot of stress."

"I know," said Kay, as she lifted up her sleeves to show Mr. Erwin the cuts on her wrist.

Mr. Erwin took a step closer towards Jay and Kay. He faced them and put his hands on their shoulders. "I know what you are going through. My sweet daughter went through the same thing. You are not alone. You must trust, trust, trust," he said. "Not in yourself but in God." Mr. Erwin then gestured his arm to all the trees lining the perimeter of the backyard. "Remember, God told Adam and Eve that they could eat from all the trees of the Garden. But what did the serpent do? He was able to create doubt that God can't be trusted and as a result got them to focus instead on the one tree they couldn't eat from. God provided abundance and the enemy was able to get them to focus on what they lacked.

"The enemy is doing the same to both of you. You both have so many God-given talents and the enemy is causing you to doubt God, doubt yourself, and focus on what you lack instead."

Jay and Kay looked at each other and then at Mr. Erwin. He could see the sadness on their faces.

"Don't let this bring you down," he said. "The enemy is very skilled at creating doubt. So skilled that he has even convinced many that God doesn't exist. Like this world and universe could somehow happen by accident. Like all of this somehow randomly and accidently came together. Somehow we are just the right distance from the sun and have just the right amount of oxygen and all the conditions and our ecosystem magically and somehow accidentally work together to create and sustain life. Come on! So many forget we are living on a liquid rock traveling through space around a great ball of fire we call the sun at 60,000 mph and spinning 1,000 mph.

"The enemy is good at convincing people to ignore God's miracles that exist all around them. So don't blame yourself. You didn't know how the battle was being waged but now you do. Now you know it starts with Doubt. The enemy knows if he can get you to doubt God you will believe his lies. And if you believe his lies you won't trust God. It's a game of deception but we are on to it. This leads us to the next D's, and they are Distort and Discourage."

Chapter 6

Distort
and Discourage

Mr. Erwin grabbed another piece of fruit from the forbidden tree and continued, "The enemy creates doubt by lying to us. He distorts truth with lies. As I told you the other day, the truth was Adam and Eve were made in God's image and the enemy convinced them they weren't. The truth was if they ate from the forbidden tree God said they would die, and the enemy said God was lying and they would not die. The enemy made it seem like God was trying to keep them from becoming like Him, when in fact God told them not to eat from the tree so they could continue to be like him. The enemy lied to them, and he continues to lie to us.

"Those negative thoughts we talked about the other day. They are lies you would never choose to think yourself. The enemy is a liar, and he's always trying to fill your mind with lies.

"Yeah, about that," said Kay. "Jay and I were talking about this the other day and it sure feels like those negative thoughts are coming from us. They are in our head, after all."

"I know it does," Mr. Erwin said as he threw the piece of fruit towards the back of the yard. "But that's how deceptive the enemy is. I don't know how it works but I know the thought comes in so fast that you think it's from you. The lie is in your head and you believe it. Then you reinforce it by repeating it to yourself. You identify with it, and it becomes a part of your identity. You may even reinforce it further by telling others. Then you feel discouraged. That's the third D. Discourage. The enemy distorts truth with lies to cause you to doubt and become discouraged.

"That's me," said Jay. "The negative thoughts get in my head, and I get so down I just want to give up. Of course I don't give up.

"Because I won't let him," interjected Kay.

"She's right," said Jay. "But while I don't give up, I beat myself up for being negative. I feel like a loser. I get mad at myself. I look in the mirror and I can't stand myself."

"I know that feeling well," said Mr. Erwin, wishing he could punch the enemy in the face but knowing that wasn't the solution. "I had the same challenges growing up. My kids did too. Here's the deal. The enemy knows he can't beat you himself. So what does he do?"

"He gets us to beat ourselves," said Kay, who was beginning to see things more clearly.

"Yep, said Mr. Erwin. "He fills our minds with lies. Lies that we aren't enough. That our future is hopeless. That we don't have what it takes to succeed. That no one loves us or will love us. That our best days are behind us. That we aren't smart enough, tall enough, good enough. That our dream won't happen. That our mistakes of the past define us."

"That we are going to mess up on stage in front of thousands of people," shouted Kay.

"That I'll never make it as a film maker," shouted Jay.

Distort and Discourage

"That life is pointless without my wife," Mr. Erwin shouted with them.

They all stood silent for a few seconds as they looked at the two trees in front of them.

"We don't give up because it's hard," Mr. Erwin said softly. "We give up because we get discouraged. The enemy lies to us so that we will make a bad choice or so that we will get discouraged and give up. And in many cases the bad choices come first, we get discouraged by the outcomes our choices produce and we give up as a result. The enemy doesn't beat us. Through the lies we believe, he gets us to beat ourselves."

"So what's the answer?" asked Kay. "I mean if those thoughts are always coming in and we can't stop them, what do we do?"

"You recognize the lies," said Mr. Erwin. "And you don't believe them. Just because you have a negative thought doesn't mean you have to believe it. Don't believe the lies. And don't beat yourself up for the thoughts in your head that are not coming from you. No more guilt, discouragement, or shame.

"That sounds good to me," said Jay as he high-fived Mr. Erwin.

"There is great freedom in knowing you are not the source of your negative thoughts," Mr. Erwin said passionately as he raised his voice. "You don't have to blame yourself anymore. You can recognize the lies, choose not to believe them, and know the positive truth. You are loved. You have value. You are worthy. You are a child of God. You are loved by God. There is a plan for your life. You have greatness inside of you and in every moment, you have the capability to do great things. The best is yet to come if you choose to believe it."

"Thanks, Mr. Erwin," said Kay as she gave him a hug while tears dripped from her eyes. Jay gave Mr. Erwin a high five. They liked hearing Mr. Erwin's words of encouragement more than the lies in their head. It certainly felt a lot better too.

"What do you say we finish for today?" asked Mr. Erwin. You two get to school and we'll talk about the last two D's tomorrow."

Distort and Discourage

"Sounds great," the twins said in unison and as they walked towards the exit of the garden. Mr. Erwin noticed that Jay walked with his back upright for the first time.

Chapter 7

Distract

Distract

As the twins walked towards Mr. Erwin's house, they noticed a nice-looking convertible sports car in the driveway. When they walked towards the two trees, they saw the forbidden tree had twenty-dollar bills attached to all the leaves. On the bench next to where Mr. Erwin sat was a basket of candy filled with bags of gummies, sours, chocolates, and chews. The twins looked at each other and just shrugged in unison.

"Whose car is that in the driveway?" asked Jay. His shoulders were slumped again and his arms were full of bruises.

"It's mine. Why are you thinking about it?" asked Mr. Erwin, with his crutches by his side.

"I don't know. I just saw it, and it looks really cool," said Jay. "I'd love to have a car like that one day."

"What's with the money on the trees and the candy?" asked Kay.

"Distractions," said Mr. Erwin. "The car, the money, the candy—they caught your attention, right?

"Yeah," said the twins at the same time.

"It's all you've been thinking about. The fourth D I want to share with you is Distract and the enemy uses distractions all the time to catch our attention and lead us away from what matters most. In the story of Adam and Eve it says that the fruit was pleasing to the eye and desirable. It looked good and she wanted it so Eve ate the fruit first and then gave it to Adam to eat and he ate as well. The enemy is a master of distraction and getting our attention with things that are pleasing to the eye and desirable but distract us from what matters most.

"It often starts out as something that seems appealing and harmless but then has a disastrous effect. It's just some candy, and the next thing you know you are addicted to sugar. It's a nice car, and then you are going into major debt to pay for it instead of investing in your future. It's just money. Next thing you know you are working harder and harder to accumulate more of it instead of spending quality time with the ones you love and who love you."

"So cars, money, and candy are bad for you," said Jay. He thought maybe candy was bad, but not money and cars.

"None of them are bad; well, maybe candy is bad for your health," Mr. Erwin said, chuckling as he looked at the fruit on the trees. "The point is that distractions are bad for you. If it's not a distraction, it's not necessarily bad. But anything that is a distraction is bad for you. Distractions are the enemy of greatness. And a distraction is anything that keeps you from what matters most.

"What matters most?" asked Kay.

"Well, let's look to the garden for the answer," said Mr. Erwin.

"First, what matters most is your relationship with God. You must focus on that more than on your desire for what may be more appealing at the time.

"Second, what matters most is becoming all that God created you to be. Distractions cause you to become less than what God created you for. It was after they ate from the forbidden tree that Adam and Eve felt afraid and ashamed. They became fearful and hid from Him in the garden.

"Third, what matters most is your relationships with others. Adam and Eve were in partnership with God and in relationship with each other but this relationship changed after they ate the fruit. Your distractions don't just hurt you; they can also hurt those you have a relationship with."

"Oh we know this well," said Kay. "Our older brother started drinking in college and next thing you know he's doing drugs and it's hurt our entire family, especially our parents. He's in rehab now."

"I'm so sorry to hear that. That's how the enemy works," said Mr. Erwin. It starts out as just a beer. Or I'll try this drug just one time. It seems fun, pleasurable, and appealing and the next thing you know you are addicted and ruining your life and hurting the people around you."

"When we were younger our Dad got distracted too," said Kay while nervously tapping her foot. "It was a friendly relationship with his assistant at work that turned into an affair. Mom found out and it almost destroyed our family. She forgave him. Dad went to work for a new company. He changed a lot for the better. Things are great now with them but we know what distractions can do." She put her arm around her brother. "That's why we want to be successful. It's why we work so hard. We want to be our best."

Jay and Kay's father had confided in Mr. Erwin years ago about what had happened so he wasn't surprised to hear the news, but he didn't think it was his place to share that with the twins.

"Yep, we all make mistakes," he said. "Distractions can lead to mistakes and failures but I also want to point out that success can be a distraction too and lead to a different kind of failure, the kind where success becomes your number one driving force. You and Jay want to be successful, and I think that's great but be careful because it can become a distraction. You might want success so bad that you focus more on that than on God. It all seems so appealing. The bright lights. The fame. The fortune. But it can be a distraction too if it keeps you from God and what matters most."

"So I shouldn't strive to be a great student and athlete?" asked Kay.

"I want to be great filmmaker," said Jay. "Is that wrong?"

"Nothing is wrong with wanting to be great," Mr. Erwin said. God made you to be great so He wants you to pursue greatness. But this pursuit must include trust and faith in Him. Your desire for God must be greater than your desire for success.

"I know way too many wealthy people who have a great career, a big house, five cars like mine, and they are absolutely miserable and disconnected from God and the important people in their life. The truth is the day we die it won't matter what kind of car we drive, how big our house is, how much money we have in the bank. What will matter is did we live the life God created us to live? Did we develop great relationships? Did we make a difference in the lives of others? At the end of their lives far too many people realize they were focused on the wrong things, but it's too late. It's not too late for both of you."

"Why do we get distracted?" asked Jay. "I don't want to end up focusing on the wrong things in my life. How do I know what's a wrong thing?"

"If it's not helping you become all God created you to be, then it's the wrong thing," said Mr. Erwin. "And sometimes the wrong thing isn't even a bad thing. There's a saying, 'If the devil won't make you bad, he'll make you busy.' He'll get you to focus on all the things that don't matter instead of what does matter. You may not do drugs, commit adultery, or hurt someone, but you may spend way too much time on social media, binge watching TV, or stay in an unhealthy relationship. You may be busy but not productive. Watching a show, playing a video game, or social media aren't bad things and if you do them in moderation that's fine. It becomes a distraction and problem when you do it too much instead of creating your life. I always told my kids: Create more than you watch."

Jay and Kay both looked at each other sheepishly, knowing they spent way too much time on their phones that were currently in their backpacks and binge-watching tv shows.

"So to answer your question, Jay, we get distracted because the enemy is good at causing us to take our focus off of God. We get distracted because the enemy clutters us with doubt, distorted lies, and discouragement, and we reach for something that is appealing; something that will make us feel better. But instead of turning to God, the ultimate source that will make us feel better, we turn to bright, shiny, appealing things, thinking they will make us feel good, but they only leave us more empty, insecure, isolated, and separate from the God who loves us and created us to be one with Him. That leads us to the fifth D, and that is Divide.

Distract

Chapter 8

Divide

Mr. Erwin stood up without using the crutches that were by his side. He asked Jay to stand next to the Tree of Life and Kay to stand next to the Tree of Knowledge of Good and Evil. "Evil's ultimate goal is to divide us and separate us from God," he said. He distracts, discourages, distorts, and creates doubt so that we will be divided from God, divided from each other and from ourselves.

Mr. Erwin then instructed Jay and Kay to take a step away from the trees and from each other towards the perimeter of the garden. He continued, "Every time you doubt God, every time you believe the lie, every time you get discouraged, and every time you get distracted you will feel further away and more disconnected from God and the people you love. Did you know the word 'anxious' literally means divided?" he asked.

He looked at Kay, who was tapping her foot on the ground. Kay looked down at her foot and for the first time realized that she was doing it.

"Is that why I'm so anxious and stressed all the time?" she asked.

"It's not the only reason," said Mr. Erwin "but it's the main reason. It's what leads to the other reasons. I'm sure you can't sleep and probably have elevated levels of stress hormones called cortisol and have developed physical and mental symptoms of anxiety and stress, but at the core of it all is the fact that you feel divided, which leads to feelings of being alone, anxious, fearful, and stressed.

"After Adam and Eve ate the fruit because of doubt, distortion, discouragement, and distraction, they were then divided from God. They felt afraid and ashamed and guilty. They actually hid from God, which is what so many do then they make bad choices. They don't run to God. They hide from Him, and as a result they feel separate and disconnected and this leads to anxiety, fear, and stress and a host of other problems.

"Why does evil want to divide us?" asked Jay.

"Because that's what evil does," said Mr. Erwin as he grabbed a leaf from the tree and ripped it in half. "It divides in order to defeat."

He then let go of both halves of the leaf and watched them fall to the ground. "Unfortunately, evil is very good at dividing and defeating us. Just look at the world today and you can see more division than ever. More people are feeling divided from God and themselves. They are dealing with stress, fear, and anxiety and giving up as a result. More families are being divided by divorce. People feel more separated from each other even though they have more ways to connect than ever. The enemy is having a field day dividing our country politically, racially, and every way possible.

"Evil is causing many to look at what makes them different instead of what they have in common. When you look at the world's problems, so many believe the lie that they are separate from each other when actually we are all one. The soul doesn't know nationality or religion or skin color.

Divide

The soul knows oneness and love. God made us to be one, and yet we allow the enemy to divide us."

Mr. Erwin grabbed another leaf from the tree and ripped it in half as Jay and Kay watched and listened.

"The enemy's main focus and goal is to divide us so it can defeat us," he repeated. "I told you that it's a spiritual battle and the enemy uses the Five D's to win the battle against God and us. When we lose this battle, it leads to the sixth D. In a marriage, this sixth D is Divorce. In a person, the sixth D is Destruction. In a team, the sixth D is Defeat. The enemy uses the Five D's to separate us from God, and this process leads to divorce, destruction, and defeat."

Jay and Kay took another step away from each other. Mr. Erwin could see the look of defeat on their faces. He knew that far too many felt hopeless when they understood the battle they were facing. It was because they were only focused on the plan against them rather than the plan to win.

"Hey you two, get over here," he said as he reached out his hands. They all held hands and formed a circle. "I told you how the enemy wins the battle," he said. "But remember, we have a choice. Adam and Eve chose to eat the fruit. They ate it because they did not believe and trust God. They believed God was withholding the best from them. They believed they would become most like God without Him. They had a choice to stay like Him or become less. They had a choice and so do we."

Mr. Erwin walked over to the Tree of Life. "There were two trees in the garden for a reason. Two trees meant that God gave them a choice and He gives us this same choice. We don't have to choose to become less. We don't have to let the enemy win. We can choose differently. God has given us a plan to win and we can choose to implement this plan. It is a plan driven by love and love always wins. I know you don't have school tomorrow but I'm here if you two want to come over.

Divide

"I have cheering practice from 10 am to 12," said Kay.

"My band practice is from 9 to 11 am," said Jay.

"Okay, how about we meet at 1 pm," said Mr. Erwin. "I'll share with you how we can overcome the Five D's and win the battle."

The Garden

Chapter 9

The Tree of Life

The next morning Jay had an amazing time at band practice. He enjoyed being at school without having to worry about getting hit or fighting in the hallways. Kay told Jay she had the most fun she's had in a long time at her practice. She was tired of being perfect. She just wanted to be happy. She still tried to be her best but didn't worry about the outcome. They decided they would tell Mr. Erwin the good news as they approached his backyard. He was standing in front of the Tree of Life when they walked up to him.

"Hey Mr. Erwin," said the twins in unison.

"Hey you two," Mr. Erwin said as he put down a bag of organic fertilizer. He decided today was the day he would no longer use the crutches. It was time to walk without them, even if that meant walking slowly and with a limp. "I told you that these two trees represented Adam and Eve's ability to choose, so let's look at the choice they had. What did each tree represent in regard to their choice?" He pointed to the forbidden tree, indicating he wanted them to start there.

"The Tree of Knowledge of Good and Evil represented the choice to do their own thing," said Kay. "I mean they could have listened to God but because they believed the lie, they chose to do what they wanted to do instead. I also think it represents the choice we have not to listen to God, not to believe him, not to trust him, and not to be in partnership with him."

"I think it represents disobedience," said Jay. "Like when my Dad tells me to do something, and I don't listen to him or follow his advice. I intentionally don't listen to him because I do what I want to do."

"And how does that usually work out?" asked Mr. Erwin.

"Not good," said Jay, as Mr. Erwin chuckled.

"You guys nailed it," he said. "I'm proud of you. The Tree of Knowledge of Good and Evil represents our choice to live life apart from God, relying on our own ability, identity, and power. It represents human striving to be perfect like God instead of living with love, peace, and joy as God's perfect creation."

"It doesn't work out too well when you do this, just like when I don't listen to my dad," said Jay.

"No it doesn't," said Mr. Erwin. "It doesn't work out because we weren't made to live apart from God. We only have limited power. We only have enough power in our lungs to blow up a balloon. God is able to expand the universe.

"Our identity is not meant to be in ourselves. For many it is and that's why they struggle so much. Identity in oneself gives rise to the EGO, which **E**dges **G**od **O**ut and leads to pride, and pride leads to our demise. When we are prideful, we think our way is better than God's way. This seems good at the time but we know it doesn't end well. That's because we weren't meant to disobey God.

75

The Tree of Life

We were meant to obey Him because God's ways are greater than our ways and His plan for our lives is greater than our plans.

"So, you have a choice to go at it alone or you can choose to live as you were created to live, and that's in an intimate relationship and partnership with God."

"Is that where the Tree of Life comes in?" asked Kay.

"Precisely," answered Mr. Erwin. "The Tree of Life represents love and trust. Would Adam and Eve love and trust God enough to solely rely on Him for their identity, significance, and purpose?" He took a piece of fruit off of the tree and ate it. "It also represents God's love and provision for Adam and Eve. All they needed was found in Him. If they had remembered this truth, they would have said NO to the evil enemy that showed up in the form of a serpent.

"That's why I believe the tree of life represents God's plan to win the battle against the enemy. When the enemy lies to us and attacks us in the place of our identity we can look at the forbidden tree, believe the lie, and take the bait. Or, we can look at the Tree of Life and remember who we truly are and whose we are and rely on and trust in God and win the battle."

Mr. Erwin grabbed two pieces of fruit from the forbidden tree and handed one to Jay and one to Kay. "What will you choose?" he asked.

Jay and Kay looked at each other and then at the fruit in their hand and simultaneously threw it towards the back of the yard.

"That's how you do it," Mr. Erwin said. "You made a choice and you must make the right one each time. This is how you win the battle. You choose the Tree of Life. You choose God. Now let's talk about some practical ways to do this and win the battle."

Chapter 10

Win the Battle

"Let's start with doubt," said Mr. Erwin as he grabbed a piece of fruit from the forbidden tree and put it in his left hand and then grabbed a piece of fruit from the Tree of Life with his right hand. "When the enemy fills your mind with doubt, the simplest, most powerful solution of all is to trust God." He held up the fruit of the forbidden tree. "Remember that the doubt isn't coming from you. Don't believe it. Trust in God. Trust that He is with you. Throughout scripture God never said it would be easy. He said,'I will be with you.' Even though you can't see him and it often feels like He is far away, you need to trust that He is walking right beside you. Trust that God has a plan for your life."

"It's easier said than done," said Jay. "It's hard to trust when you feel like everything in life is against you and you don't feel like God is on your side."

"I know, I know," said Mr. Erwin empathetically. "This is why so many don't trust. They look at their circumstances rather than to God. They look at their challenges rather than to God, who will help them overcome their challenges. Many say, 'Show me God and I will trust you.' But it works the other way. When you trust, God will show you."

"Not always right away," said Kay. "Sometimes I pray, and it's like God isn't listening."

"You are right," said Mr. Erwin. "It feels like that often, and it can be scary and discouraging. At times we feel abandoned. But that's because we want God to work according to our timeline instead of His. We want God to be like FedEx and deliver overnight. But some miracles take time." He chuckled as he threw the fruit from the forbidden tree away. "I think in those moments God is testing our faith. What will we choose?

"When you are doubting God and believing He can't be trusted, the enemy has you right where he wants you. You are on your way to losing the battle. That's why no matter what doubt says, you must trust in God and trust that He has the best in store for you. No matter what your circumstances are, you need to trust in God's plan. When it seems like God has abandoned you, trust. When you don't feel like trusting, trust. Trust in the one who created you. Trust in the one who walks with you. Trust in the one who loves you. Trust in the one who has a plan for your life and gives you hope and a future. When your trust is greater than your doubt, you are on your way to winning the battle."

Kay had tears in her eyes as she thought about all the times she doubted and didn't trust. Hearing that God loved her and was walking with her opened a tiny crack in her heart and she felt something she hadn't felt in a long time. It had been so long she had forgotten what it felt like and remembered what it was. It was love.

"I'm going to trust from now on," she said. "I know there will be times the doubt will be so strong it will be hard to trust but I'm going to do my best."

"Me too," said Jay, who was comforted by the thought that his challenges didn't mean God was abandoning him but rather testing him. "I've been angry at God for a while. I thought he hated me," as his eyes welled up with tears. "Now I know he was giving me a choice to test me."

"Yes, he was," Mr. Erwin said in a soft, comforting tone. "You were angry at God, thinking he hated you, when really he's been testing you to make you stronger. He's not doing something to you. He's working through you, and you will see this clearly when you look back on your life. When you are older and making films and dealing with rejection and bullies in the industry, you will be stronger for what you have been going through now."

"I get it," said Jay as he looked at the cut on his hand. He was getting stronger and was no longer allowing himself to be a punching bag.

"And remember," said Mr. Erwin. "Trust is not a one-time thing. You don't just trust once. You have to keep trusting. The enemy will keep lying to you and trying to get you to believe his lies. He's always lurking and often waits until those moments when you are lonely, hungry, insecure, emotionally weak from a difficult circumstance in your life. That's when he plants those seeds of doubt the most. *Are you sure you can Trust God? Does God really want the best for you? Why would God do this to you?* Sometimes it's just a subtle thought. Other times it feels like you are being bombarded. But make no mistake: his goal is the same."

"Is there something we can do when those lies fill our minds?" asked Kay. "They can be pretty loud."

"I'm glad you asked that," said Mr. Erwin. "I want to share with you a powerful strategy that will help you. It's from a friend of mine named Dr. James Gills. He accomplished the amazing feat of completing six double Ironman Triathlons, which means you do an Ironman and the next day you do another one. And the last time he did it he was 59 years old.

"When he was asked how he did it, he said,'I've learned to talk to myself instead of listen to myself. If I listen to myself, I hear all the complaints and doubts and reasons why I can't finish the race. I'm too old and tired and my legs feel like they are going to collapse. But if I talk to myself, I feed myself with the words and encouragement that I need to keep going and finish the race.' He would memorize and recite scripture and that's what fueled him. You can do the same. But instead of the phrase *Listen to yourself* I would say *Don't listen to the enemy's lies* because as we discussed those *thoughts aren't coming from you*. So don't listen to the lies. Don't believe the lies. And then do one other thing."

"What's that?" asked Jay, who was hanging on every word. He desperately needed a way to counter the negative thoughts in his head.

"Speak truth to the lies," said Mr. Erwin. "Talk to yourself and speak words of truth and encouragement to counter the lies."

"What is truth?" asked Kay. She had believed the lies for so long that she had come to believe the lies were her truth.

"Truth is what God says about you," answered Mr. Erwin. "Truth is who you truly are. As I told you the other day, you are a child of God. That's truth. You are loved by God. That's truth. You were born with greatness inside of you, to do great things.

That's truth. The power within you is more powerful than the circumstances around you. That's truth."

Mr. Erwin grabbed two pads of paper he had sitting on the bench and gave one to Kay and one to Jay. "What I want you to do is write down on the left side of the paper all the lies that often fill your mind. Then on the right side I want you to write down a truth that you will speak to the lie."

"Can you give an example?" asked Kay.

"Sure," said Mr. Erwin. "On the left side you might write down the lie that 'I have to perform well in cheering in order to be worthy and receive love and recognition from others.' On the right side you would write, 'I'm worthy because God says I'm worthy. I'm already loved. I'm free to give my all to be my best without tying my self-worth to the outcome."

"That feels good," said Kay. "I did something like this at practice this morning and it worked."

"It should," said Mr. Erwin. "When truth exposes and replaces a lie, you always feel better and perform better."

"What about me?" asked Jay.

"For you, Jay," said Mr. Erwin, "a lie you would write down is that your future as a filmmaker is hopeless. The truth you would write on the right-hand side of the paper is that God has a plan for your life and career, and the future is always full of hope."

The twins then proceeded to write down their lies and truths on the paper. When they finished Mr. Erwin said, "Make sure you keep that and look at it often until you have memorized them. Then whenever those lies come in, speak truth to the lie, especially when you start to get discouraged. Remember the enemy distorts truth with lies in order to discourage you. The third D is Discourage, and when you get discouraged you are more likely to give up and be defeated. That's why you must encourage yourself and others.

"Instead of feeling discouraged, you must continually encourage. Encouragement is like oxygen for your mind, heart, and soul. You need to consistently encourage yourself and others with

88

The Garden

God's truth in order to win the battle. It's what Jesus did when he was in the wilderness and he gives us the blueprint to win the battle."

Mr. Erwin walked over to a bronze statue that was behind the two trees. It was a statue of Jesus washing the feet of one of his disciples. He pointed to it and said, "I didn't know much about Jesus until after my wife passed away but when I learned how he overcame the enemy in the wilderness, I knew he had a message I needed to hear.

"You see, in the wilderness the enemy lied to and tempted him. And each time the enemy did that, Jesus quoted scripture from the Old Testament and spoke truth to the lie. Each time the enemy tried to distort the truth and create doubt and discourage him, Jesus responded with God's truth. Thousands of years ago he was showing us how to win the battle today. It wasn't some ethereal teaching to get us to escape the reality of life on earth. He gave us a practical application on how to win the battle everyone is facing right here, right now. It's not just meant for Christians. It's meant for everyone.

In the Garden Adam and Eve believed the lie and lost. In the wilderness Jesus spoke truth to the lie and won. And we can do the same."

"How come Adam and Eve got distracted and Jesus didn't?" asked Kay.

"Because Adam and Eve didn't focus on what mattered most and Jesus did," answered Mr. Erwin. "That's how you overcome the fourth D of Distraction. You focus on what matters most, and as I told you the other day, what matters most is your relationship with God, becoming all God created you to be and your relationship with others. And when we talk about relationships, what are we really talking about?" He paused and waited for the answer as Jay and Kay tapped their heads as if that would make the answer come quicker.

Then the answer came. It was as if Jay heard the word in his head. "Love," he shouted. "Relationships are all about love."

"Yes," said Mr. Erwin. "It's so simple and powerful that we forget what really matters most. Thankfully Jesus made it simple and gave us a practical application once again. When he was asked about which of all the laws and commandments were the most important, he distilled it down to two commandments and one message. Love. Jesus said, *Love your Lord your God with all your heart, with all your soul, with all your mind and with all your strength*. Then he said, *Love your neighbor as yourself. There is no commandment greater than these.*"

"All you need is love," said Jay, who loved his grandparents favorite music as much as he did modern music.

"Jesus and the Beatles were right," chuckled Mr. Erwin. "When the enemy tries to distract you with things that are bad, remember what matters most: Your relationship with God. Loving, honoring, and obeying Him and becoming all you are meant to be. When you are filled with fear, remember to focus on God's love. In the Bible, Jesus said *Fear not* over 300 times because He knew our focus needed to be on God's love, not our fear. God's perfect love casts out fear. So when you are focused on love, fear has no power over you. When the enemy tries to distract you with fear and things that don't matter, remember it all comes down to love. Love God, love yourself, love people. If you focus on loving God and loving others, you will become a powerful force that not only overcomes the Five D's but you will make a greater difference in the world.

"As I told you the other day, so many things seem bright and shiny and appealing, but the only thing that will fill you up, the only thing your soul longs for is a relationship with God and a loving relationship with others. That's what matters the most above all things. If God is filling you up, you don't need any other artificial source to feel good. Love is the most powerful force in the universe. Love is what connects you and God. It connects you to each other. It connects you to yourself. This leads us to the way you overcome the fifth D of Divide and win the battle. It is to unite."

Chapter 11

Love Wins

"You said love wins," Jay reminded him.

"Yes, it does," said Mr. Erwin. "Love wins because Love unites. Evil's main goal is to divide you and separate you from God. Yet we know God loves you and created you to be one with and united with Him. When you are united, you can't be divided. When you are united, you are strong."

"How do we become united with God?" asked Kay as she tapped her foot nervously. "I don't feel united very often. I often feel separate from God."

"I feel the same way," said Jay as he sighed and took a deep breath. "I often feel depressed and worried about everything. I hate worrying but I can't stop it."

"I know the feeling," said Mr. Erwin. "After my wife passed away, I was carrying a heavy burden. I felt very anxious and divided. I was angry at God and wasn't sure I wanted to even live anymore. I didn't care about life and yet felt anxious about life. I was like, why am I anxious if I don't care?"

"So what did you do?" asked Kay, who was feeling more anxious as they talked.

"It's not what I did that helped," he answered. "It's what God did for me. You see, I tried to meditate, but that didn't seem to calm my restless, anxious, and angry heart. I know it works for a lot of people but I tried that and everything you can think of and nothing worked. Then one day I walked past the bookshelf and saw my wife's favorite books and something told me to read the one by Erwin McManus. I liked his first name so I picked it up and started reading it.

"It was about Jesus and it spoke to me. My wife always wanted me to go to church with her but I wouldn't go. I wasn't interested. After I read this book, I started listening to some of her favorite sermons. Many of them talked about this battle we are facing. They saw it so clearly while everyone else seemed oblivious to what was going on. Then I learned that Jesus's life and purpose is the answer to what happened in the garden.

"You see, what happened in the garden gets reconciled on the cross. What happened in the garden represents man's separation from God. Jesus represents man's unity, oneness, and reconciliation with God. Jesus died to unite man back to God. Evil thought it had won and God said *not so fast*. Then Jesus showed up and everything changed. It all made perfect sense. The pieces of the puzzle and two stories that were told thousands of years apart fit too perfectly together to be an accident. My friend Rich Villodas said it best, 'Adam and Eve hid behind a tree, naked and covered in shame. Then Jesus hung on a tree, naked and conquered shame.' The cross of Jesus is the great reversal. What was lost was now won. In the battle of good and evil, long before there was Superman, Wonder Woman, Luke Skywalker, and the Black Panther fighting evil with good, there was Jesus fighting evil for us and in his death on the cross, we won."

"Why did he have to die?" asked Jay. "Most superheroes don't die."

"Because the ultimate hero sacrifices for those they love. Because true love is sacrificial. Because God wanted us to know how much he loves us. In the battle of good versus evil, Jesus didn't just come to give us the practical answers. He came to be the answer. He came to unite and restore what had been divided and destroyed in the garden. The serpent represents the evil enemy we face. Jesus is God's love and truth. And as I said before, love wins. What evil intended for bad, God used for good."

"If Jesus wins, then how come so many Christians suffer from depression and anxiety and make bad choices and engage in evil acts?" asked Kay. Her family had gone to church since they were kids and she saw that the people closest to her were often losing the battle.

"Because knowing the story and living it are two different things," he answered. "The enemy deceives them just like he deceives everyone. He causes them to forget who they are. They need to remember these truths as much as everyone. This isn't about religion. God isn't a religion. He is a relationship. Jesus didn't come for Christians. He came for everyone to be united to God. He's not a club you join. He's the love you invite into your heart that unites you with your creator who created you for a relationship with Him. Life is about inviting and receiving this love that transforms you from the inside out and gives you the power to take on the enemy and win the battle."

"After my dad messed up, he said he asked my mom to forgive him and then he asked God to forgive him," said Kay. "He told us that God did forgive him and over time we saw him change in a lot of ways."

"He did," confirmed Jay. "You could tell there was something different about him. We used to go to church and he would look around. But now I saw him pray, I mean really pray. Like he was talking to God and God was talking back."

"The same thing happened to me," said Mr. Erwin. "I too discovered the power of prayer and it changed my life. I always believed in God but never had much of a relationship with Him. When I prayed more, I found that prayer changes you more than it changes God. You don't do it because God needs your prayers. You do it because you need God. The more I prayed and read about Jesus and believed in what Jesus came to do for me and for us, my relationship with Him became deeper and more intimate. My heart opened and all of a sudden I started receiving all these insights I'm sharing with you. I felt more peace and love and joy. Even though I missed my wife, I was no longer angry. I believed in God and His plan and saw that there was so much more going on than what we see in front of us. I recognized the battle that was going on and saw that Jesus was the only one who came to help me win the battle.

He not only saw evil and recognized it, he came to defeat it.

"As a result, I was no longer fighting a battle with one hand tied behind my back. I was no longer losing the battle by myself. I was winning it with Jesus. I wasn't trying to go at it alone anymore. I knew I wasn't strong enough. My identity was not in myself. I was now aligned with God. My identity was found in Him. I was a child of God and I was free to experience a life of freedom, love, peace, and joy." Mr. Erwin then walked over to the statue of Jesus and said, "And let me tell you, there's no better feeling."

"I want to feel that," said Kay. "I'm tired of fighting this battle alone."

"Me too," said Jay. "I don't want to die anymore. I want to live life to the fullest."

"Well, then come over here," said Mr. Erwin, with a smile on his face. He reached out his hands, and they grabbed them and formed a circle around the statue of Jesus. "I'm glad you said you want to live life to the fullest, because Jesus didn't come to condemn or judge anyone. He came so that you would live life to the fullest. In this spirit, all you have to do is give your burdens, your pain, your anxiety, your fears, your stress, and your past to Jesus. You say I give it all to you Jesus. I give you my life. When you say this, God provides an exchange. You give him your life and your burden and pain, and He gives you His Life and Spirit. He unites you to Himself, and you become one. What was separated is now united. Victory is yours."

Mr. Erwin paused and looked at their faces. He saw how the battle had weakened them and yet also realized that it brought them to this very moment. You try to fight it on your own and when you realize you aren't strong enough you become open to a greater strength. Most, unfortunately, don't know this greater strength is available to them. "Are you ready? Do you want to try it?" he asked.

Jay and Kay nodded in unison and said the simple prayer together. Then something happened. It was something they couldn't explain. It was something that you couldn't understand until you experienced it yourself. They started to cry and then they started to weep. They couldn't stop. It was as if all their fears, stress, anxiety, and pain that had been bottled up inside them were being released at once. The flood gates opened and everything came pouring out and what was left was something that was always there. It was the eternal love of God that they were now able to feel.

Mr. Erwin hugged both of them with an arm around each. When the tears subsided, they decided to meet again tomorrow afternoon. He told them this was just the beginning of a deeper conversation they would be having with God throughout their life but it was an important moment they should never forget.

And as Jay and Kay walked out of the backyard, Mr. Erwin knew it was a moment that would make all the rest of their moments more meaningful and abundant. Words wouldn't be able to explain it. They would have to experience it to know it. Like his favorite chocolate cake at the café down the street. You could tell someone about the cake but they wouldn't know how good it was until they ate it. If you never ate the chocolate cake, you wouldn't understand what people who had the cake were talking about when they talked about it. Some might even think you were crazy for loving the cake so much. But those who ate the cake knew how good it was and would be able to understand and share in the power of that experience.

Chapter 12

Victory Is Yours

When Jay and Kay arrived in the garden, they saw Mr. Erwin polishing the statue as he sat on the ground beside it. "How do you feel?" he asked them, knowing what they were going to say.

"We were emotionally drained and exhausted last night," said Kay.

"But we feel great this morning," said Jay. "We feel lighter and freer like I feel on the days I don't have to carry my band instrument around."

"Victory feels good," said Mr. Erwin. He stopped polishing the statue, put the rag down, and stood up. He noticed that Jay wasn't slumping as much and Kay wasn't tapping her foot nervously. "I want you to remember this feeling. I want you to remember that you are victorious."

"How could we forget it?" asked Jay. He thought he could never forget how good he felt.

"Oh, it happens," said Mr. Erwin. "It happens a lot to a lot of people. Over time the enemy continues to try to make you forget the battle has been won. The enemy gets you to focus on the mistakes you made in the past rather than the victory that is yours. When you make a new mistake or fall short of perfection, he'll try to make you feel like a fraud. He'll try to make you feel like you didn't earn this victory. And before you know it, you're walking around all defeated again."

"So even though we are victorious and won the battle, it's not over?" asked Jay, who was trying to understand how they could be victorious and yet have to continue to withstand the attacks of the enemy.

"Here's the deal," said Mr. Erwin. "You are victorious. You must walk in that victory. Yet, you will have to prepare for new attacks. And as you fight new battles you can do so knowing you have won the battle before it even starts. You are not fighting for victory. You are fighting

The Garden

from victory. You know the full story. You know what happened in the garden is redeemed. What was once lost is now won. You didn't earn this victory yourself but don't let the enemy distort this truth and use it against you.

"Instead, realize that's the beauty and amazing thing about Jesus. You didn't earn it but victory is yours. That's what grace is all about. That's what love does. It gives you what you couldn't do on your own. So you should walk around confident but humble. Humble knowing there is a God and it's not you. Confident knowing you were made in God's image, and He has a plan for your life and provided a way for you to be victorious.

"Yes, the battle keeps playing out over and over again. It will happen in your life and all those on the planet. The enemy will continue to create doubt, distortion, discouragement, distraction, and division. But your job is to remember that victory is yours. Don't allow yourself to get defeated. Remember how to counter the Five D's. Remember who you are. Find your identity in God, not in what others think or say about you. Also, don't let your identity be defined by the world or what the world can provide you.

"Remember everything you need, God will provide. When your identity, reliance, and trust is found in God alone and not yourself you will continue to be victorious. Jesus won the battle for you but you must choose to receive this victory every day. When you do it will lead to the seventh D and that is your Destiny."

"So if we don't overcome the Five D's it leads to the sixth D, which is Defeat," said Kay. "But in winning the battle each day, it leads us to overcome the Five D's and avoid the sixth D and leads us to the seventh D, which is our Destiny."

"You got it, Kay. And here's the cool thing. Seven is the number of completion. The seventh D is Destiny and this is the plan and purpose God has for you. You are not here by accident. You are loved and there is a plan for your life. And like any hero in an epic movie, you must overcome evil with good in order to realize it. So God gives you your life, He allows you to face struggles and challenges along the way, but most importantly He gives you the power of choice, a plan and a way to overcome evil in order to live the life you were created to live and fulfill your destiny. God's fruit is Destiny, not divorce, defeat, and destruction. What the enemy meant for evil, God meant for good.

"So be confident that victory is yours and yet walk humbly each day, relying on God to receive this victory. After all, when Superman took off his superman outfit, who was he?"

"He was Clark Kent," answered Jay. "Everyone knows that."

"Actually, that's not true," answered Mr. Erwin with a smirk. "He was still Superman. He was Superman on the inside. It didn't matter what he was wearing. The same goes for you throughout the rest of your life. No matter what career you choose or role you play in the world or what clothes you wear to work, you are still a child of God on the inside and you have the greatest power in the universe."

"What's that?" asked Jay.

"The power of love to overcome your fear, stress, and challenges," said Mr. Erwin. "And like every superhero, you will have to fight new battles and face new challenges. But as you do, always know that I'm here for you to coach you along the way. The stakes are higher than soccer matches when you were kids, and I'm here to help you win."

Chapter 13

New Challenges and Victories

Mr. Erwin and the twins agreed to meet in the garden before school once a week going forward. It was a time they both looked forward to, to talk about any challenges they were facing, and how the Five D's were showing up in their lives and what they needed to do to counter them.

As is always the case, new challenges emerged, but instead of causing the twins to go down the spiral staircase of worry and despair, they were armored with the truth and plan to win the new battles they faced. Jay still faced the bullies but he stopped walking like he was defeated and started walking with confidence. Eventually they got tired of Jay hitting back and left him alone. At times, Jay still worried about his future but Mr. Erwin would remind him not to worry about his greatness in the future. Just be great today. God will take care of the outcome. As a result, Jay spent less time worrying about being a famous filmmaker and more time focusing on making great movies. He posted them online and one just happened to be seen by a professor at a film school that offered Jay a scholarship. His grades still weren't great but his films were, and he was more clear about his purpose and less worried about his future than ever.

Despite all the victories he was experiencing, that didn't stop him from having suicidal thoughts when his girlfriend broke up with him. Jay met her his junior year in high school. It turns out when you know who you truly are, others are more drawn to you and want to know you. A girl who loved music and film as much as he did talked to him after band practice one day and after that they were inseparable. Until the day she got accepted into her dream school, knew she didn't want to be in a long-distance relationship, and cheated on him with one of their friends. All of Jay's past fears and insecurities came roaring back, and he was filled with doubt, discouragement, and thoughts of ending it all to avoid the pain.

Thankfully, Mr. Erwin was able to help him see how he was being attacked once again and reminded him that God has a plan. If she was the one for him it would work out. If not, it meant there was someone else that God has for him, and he would meet her in the right place at the right time.

Jay realized how easy it was to forget the lessons of the Five D's and get discouraged and defeated. At first his ex-girlfriend's actions made him feel like something was wrong with him. It made him question himself. Was something wrong with him that she would do this to him? His identity was being attacked. Mr. Erwin helped him see that her actions had nothing to do with him. His identity should never be defined by what others say or do but rather by the God who created you. The experience made Jay rely more on God and develop a deeper, more trusting relationship with Him. He found more focus for his films and more peace when thinking about what the future held.

Kay stopped wearing long-sleeved shirts when the cuts healed on her arms. While the light scars were still there, they served as a good reminder of the fear and anxiety that had sabotaged her in the past and the truth that had set her free. Mr. Erwin went to watch her cheering competitions with her dad and mom and could tell she felt free when cheering and no longer worried what people were thinking.

Mr. Erwin encouraged her to perform for an audience of one, the one who created and loved her no matter how she performed. Each performance she remembered him telling her that God doesn't call us to be perfect. He calls us to be faithful and trust in His perfect plan for our imperfect life. It would be advice she would need to draw upon when she tore her ACL at the end of her junior year. At the time it seemed like her dream of cheering in college at one of the finest schools in the country was over. She struggled with doubt and even though she told herself God had a plan, that didn't stop the fear and anxiety from resurfacing.

But with Mr. Erwin's help and their weekly talks she didn't let the fear and anxiety take hold. She prayed often for help, for strength, for guidance, and for a miracle. It was a long year of uncertainty and rehab but she made it back to the stage her senior year. The experience taught her patience and trust and leadership. She couldn't perform while she was injured so she learned to help her team by encouraging them and discovered her leadership voice in the process.

Her desire to be successful was replaced with a desire to serve and lead her team. The difference was less stress and more passion, and when she cheered with her team again, she did so with more joy and faith. In the past she cheered with the hope it would get her into her dream school. But now she cheered because she loved it and loved her team. She ended up getting into a great college. It wasn't her dream school but she knew it was the right school for her and received the academic scholarship she had worked so hard for. And just when she thought her cheering career was over, she received a call from the college cheering coach, letting her know she could try out as a walk-on if she wanted to. She told Mr. Erwin if it was meant to be and was part of God's plan, it would happen. She wasn't worried about it. She knew who she was and trusted God knew what was best for her and her future.

Mr. Erwin loved seeing the twins take on their challenges with optimism, hope, faith, belief, and trust. They knew the battle they faced but weren't scared of it. They walked and talked like champions who knew they were victorious and would eventually overcome any setback they faced. No longer would they allow fear to paralyze them, anxiety to control them, or stress to sabotage them. They knew they were in a battle. They knew the enemy's game plan. And they knew how to counter it. They had become great students. But what impressed him most is when they showed up one day to teach him something.

Chapter 14

The 8th D

After high school graduation, before Mr. Erwin took his summer trip to the mountains, the twins arrived at his house with their older brother. Damon had just gotten out of rehab. It was his second time there because he had started using drugs again after his first visit. The twins wanted him to meet Mr. Erwin and found him in the backyard.

"Hey Mr. Erwin," said Kay. "We want you to meet our older brother, Damon."

Mr. Erwin put the watering hose down and reached out and shook Damon's hand and said hello. He looked into his eyes and could tell he had been fighting a losing battle for a while.

"Do you want me to tell him about the story of Adam and Eve in the Garden?" he asked, expecting Jay and Kay to say yes.

"Actually, we already told him the story," said Kay.

"And we told him about the Five D's," said Jay.

"We brought him here because we wanted to thank you for teaching us, so that way we could teach him," said Kay. "It's helping him a lot."

"It is," said Damon. "It's very eye opening. Now I know why I've been losing the battle. And I'm grateful I now have a plan to win. Who would have thought my younger brother and sister would have the answers I needed?"

"It's the answers we all need," said Mr. Erwin.

"Yeah, that's also why we are here," said Kay. "We believe everyone needs to learn what you taught us, so we decided there needed to be an eighth D."

"What's the eighth D?" asked Mr. Erwin curiously.

"It's Disciple," said Jay. "Once you learn about the Five D's and how to win the battle that will lead you to your Destiny then it's important that you share it with others to disciple them. Your destiny is never about yourself. Every hero knows they were made for others, to help others, and it's about taking action to do this."

"Disciple as a verb means to teach," said Kay. "You learn it and then you teach it to those you want to help."

"Like me," said Damon.

"I love that," said Mr. Erwin. "Thank you for teaching me this. I guess it's fitting then that I got you these for your graduation." He reached into his pocket and held up an identical coin in each hand. On one side of the coin it had the Five D's and on the other side it had the way to overcome each D. It looked like this:

"I was originally giving these to you so when you go off to college you wouldn't forget these lessons.

But now I know I was supposed to give them to you so you can disciple and help others as well. I can't wait to hear about all the people you encourage and see the difference you make."

"We're excited," said Kay. "We know it won't be easy. The enemy doesn't want these simple truths out there so he will create a lot of doubt, distortion, and distraction and do whatever it can to stop us from sharing and reaching people. It will be a challenge for sure, but we know this is our purpose and we had to go through the battle in order to help others win it."

"We are stronger for it," said Jay.

"Yes you are. I'm so proud of you both," said Mr. Erwin as he pointed to all the trees and paused with tears in his eyes. Then he grabbed a piece of fruit from the Tree of Life. "And don't forget to keep nourishing yourselves as you seek to help others. Your mind and soul is like a garden. You need to weed the negative and feed the positive each day. If you do it just one time it won't do much. But if you weed and feed the garden of your mind and soul for a week, a month, a year, seven years, and a lifetime, your garden will look magnificent and you'll produce amazing fruit."

Mr. Erwin looked at the piece of fruit in his hand and then took a big bite out of it, smiled, and said, "And always remember, whatever you are going through keep believing the best is yet to come. God has a plan!"

The End.

About the Author

Jon Gordon is a husband, father, author, and speaker who has inspired millions of readers around the world. He is the author of 20 books, including eight bestsellers: *The Energy Bus, The Carpenter, Training Camp, You Win in the Locker Room First, The Power of Positive Leadership, The Power of a Positive Team, The Coffee Bean,* and *Stay Positive*. He is passionate about developing positive leaders, organizations, and teams. Connect with Jon at JonGordon.com.

Other Books by Jon Gordon

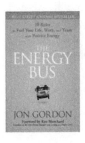

The Energy Bus

A man whose life and career are in shambles learns from a unique bus driver and set of passengers how to overcome adversity. Enjoy an enlightening ride of positive energy that is improving the way leaders lead, employees work, and teams function.

www.TheEnergyBus.com

The No Complaining Rule

Follow a VP of Human Resources who must save herself and her company from ruin and discover proven principles and an actionable plan to win the battle against individual and organizational negativity.

www.NoComplainingRule.com

Training Camp

This inspirational story about a small guy with a big heart, and a special coach who guides him on a quest for excellence, reveals the 11 winning habits that separate the best individuals and teams from the rest.

www.TrainingCamp11.com

The Shark and the Goldfish

Delightfully illustrated, this quick read is packed with tips and strategies on how to respond to challenges beyond your control in order to thrive during waves of change.

www.SharkandGoldfish.com

Soup

The newly appointed CEO of a popular soup company is brought in to reinvigorate the brand and bring success back to a company that has fallen on hard times. Through her journey, discover the key ingredients to unite, engage, and inspire teams to create a culture of greatness.

www.Soup11.com

The Seed

Go on a quest for the meaning and passion behind work with Josh, an up-and-comer at his company who is disenchanted with his job. Through Josh's cross-country journey, you'll find surprising new sources of wisdom and inspiration in your own business and life.

www.Seed11.com

One Word

One Word is a simple concept that delivers powerful life change! This quick read will inspire you to simplify your life and work by focusing on just one word for this year. *One Word* creates clarity, power, passion, and life-change. When you find your word, live it, and share it, your life will become more rewarding and exciting than ever.

www.getoneword.com

133

Other Books by Jon Gordon

The Positive Dog

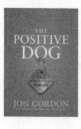

We all have two dogs inside of us. One dog is positive, happy, optimistic, and hopeful. The other dog is negative, mad, pessimistic, and fearful. These two dogs often fight inside us, but guess who wins? The one you feed the most. *The Positive Dog* is an inspiring story that not only reveals the strategies and benefits of being positive, but also an essential truth: being positive doesn't just make you better; it makes everyone around you better.

www.feedthepositivedog.com

The Carpenter

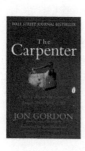

The Carpenter is Jon Gordon's most inspiring book yet—filled with powerful lessons and success strategies. Michael wakes up in the hospital with a bandage on his head and fear in his heart after collapsing during a morning jog. When Michael finds out the man who saved his life is a carpenter, he visits him and quickly learns that he is more than just a carpenter; he is also a builder of lives, careers, people, and teams. In this journey, you will learn timeless principles to help you stand out, excel, and make an impact on people and the world.

www.carpenter11.com

The Hard Hat

A true story about Cornell lacrosse player George Boiardi, *The Hard Hat* is an unforgettable book about a selfless, loyal, joyful, hardworking, competitive, and compassionate leader and teammate, the impact he had on his team and program, and the lessons we can learn from him. This inspirational story will teach you how to build a great team and be the best teammate you can be.

www.hardhat21.com

You Win in the Locker Room First

Based on the extraordinary experiences of NFL Coach Mike Smith and leadership expert Jon Gordon, *You Win in the Locker Room First* offers a rare behind-the-scenes look at one of the most pressure-packed leadership jobs on the planet, and what leaders can learn from these experiences in order to build their own winning teams.

www.wininthelockerroom.com

Other Books by Jon Gordon

Life Word

Life Word reveals a simple, powerful tool to help you identify the word that will inspire you to live your best life while leaving your greatest legacy. In the process, you'll discover your *why*, which will help show you how to live with a renewed sense of power, purpose, and passion.

www.getoneword.com/lifeword

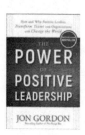

The Power of Positive Leadership

The Power of Positive Leadership is your personal coach for becoming the leader your people deserve. Jon Gordon gathers insights from his best-selling fables to bring you the definitive guide to positive leadership. Difficult times call for leaders who are up to the challenge. Results are the by-product of your culture, teamwork, vision, talent, innovation, execution, and commitment. This book shows you how to bring it all together to become a powerfully positive leader.

www.powerofpositiveleadership.com

The Power of a Positive Team

In *The Power of a Positive Team*, Jon Gordon draws upon his unique team building experience, as well as conversations with some of the greatest teams in history, to provide an essential framework of proven practices to empower teams to work together more effectively and achieve superior results.

www.PowerOfAPositiveTeam.com

The Coffee Bean

From best-selling author Jon Gordon and rising star Damon West comes *The Coffee Bean*: an illustrated fable that teaches readers how to transform their environment, overcome challenges, and create positive change.

www.coffeebeanbook.com

Stay Positive

Fuel yourself and others with positive energy—inspirational quotes and encouraging messages to live by from best-selling author, Jon Gordon. Keep this little book by your side, read from it each day, and feed your mind, body, and soul with the power of positivity.

www.StayPositiveBook.com

Other Books by Jon Gordon

The Energy Bus for Kids

The illustrated children's adaptation of the best-selling book *The Energy Bus* tells the story of George, who, with the help of his school bus driver, Joy, learns that if he believes in himself, he'll find the strength to overcome any challenge. His journey teaches kids how to overcome negativity, bullies, and everyday challenges to be their best.

www.EnergyBusKids.com

Thank You and Good Night

Thank You and Good Night is a beautifully illustrated book that shares the heart of gratitude. Jon Gordon takes a little boy and girl on a fun-filled journey from one perfect moonlit night to the next. During their adventurous days and nights, the children explore the people, places, and things they are thankful for.

The Hard Hat for Kids

The Hard Hat for Kids is an illustrated guide to teamwork. Adapted from the best-seller *The Hard Hat*, this uplifting story presents practical insights and life-changing lessons that are immediately applicable to everyday situations, giving kids—and adults—a new outlook on cooperation, friendship, and the selfless nature of true teamwork.

www.HardHatforKids.com

Other Books by Jon Gordon

One Word for Kids

If you could choose only one word to help you have your best year ever, what would it be? *Love? Fun? Believe? Brave?* It's probably different for each person. How you find your word is just as important as the word itself. And once you know your word, what do you do with it? In *One Word for Kids*, best-selling author Jon Gordon—along with coauthors Dan Britton and Jimmy Page—asks these questions to children and adults of all ages, teaching an important life lesson in the process.

www.getoneword.com/kids